THE LIFE CYCLE OF A
Frog

By Colleen Sexton

BELLWETHER MEDIA • MINNEAPOLIS, MN

BLASTOFF!
READERS
3

Note to Librarians, Teachers, and Parents:

Blastoff! Readers are carefully developed by literacy experts and combine standards-based content with developmentally appropriate text.

Level 1 provides the most support through repetition of high-frequency words, light text, predictable sentence patterns, and strong visual support.

Level 2 offers early readers a bit more challenge through varied simple sentences, increased text load, and less repetition of high-frequency words.

Level 3 advances early-fluent readers toward fluency through increased text and concept load, less reliance on visuals, longer sentences, and more literary language.

Level 4 builds reading stamina by providing more text per page, increased use of punctuation, greater variation in sentence patterns, and increasingly challenging vocabulary.

Level 5 encourages children to move from "learning to read" to "reading to learn" by providing even more text, varied writing styles, and less familiar topics.

Whichever book is right for your reader, Blastoff! Readers are the perfect books to build confidence and encourage a love of reading that will last a lifetime!

This edition first published in 2010 by Bellwether Media, Inc.

No part of this publication may be reproduced in whole or in part without written permission of the publisher. For information regarding permission, write to Bellwether Media, Inc., Attention: Permissions Department, 5357 Penn Avenue South, Minneapolis, MN 55419.

Library of Congress Cataloging-in-Publication Data
Sexton, Colleen A., 1967–
   The life cycle of a frog / by Colleen Sexton.
      p. cm. — (Blastoff! Readers life cycles)
   Includes bibliographical references and index.
   Summary: "Developed by literacy experts for students in kindergarten through grade three, this book follows frogs as they transform from eggs to adults. Through leveled text and related images, young readers will watch these creatures grow through every stage of life"—Provided by publisher.
   ISBN 978-1-60014-308-3 (hardcover : alk. paper)
   1. Frogs—Life cycles—Juvenile literature. I. Title.
   QL668.E2S49 2010
   597.8'9—dc22

                        2009037263

Printed in the United States of America, North Mankato, MN.
010110   1149

Contents

Frogs are **amphibians** that live near ponds, lakes, and rivers.

They spend their lives on land and in the water.

Frogs grow in stages. The stages of a frog's **life cycle** are egg, **tadpole**, and adult.

adult

egg

tadpole

The life cycle begins in spring. A male frog **croaks** a song. A female chooses him as a **mate**.

The female lays thousands of eggs in the water. The male **fertilizes** the eggs.

The mass of eggs is called **spawn**.
Clear jelly surrounds each egg in
the spawn.

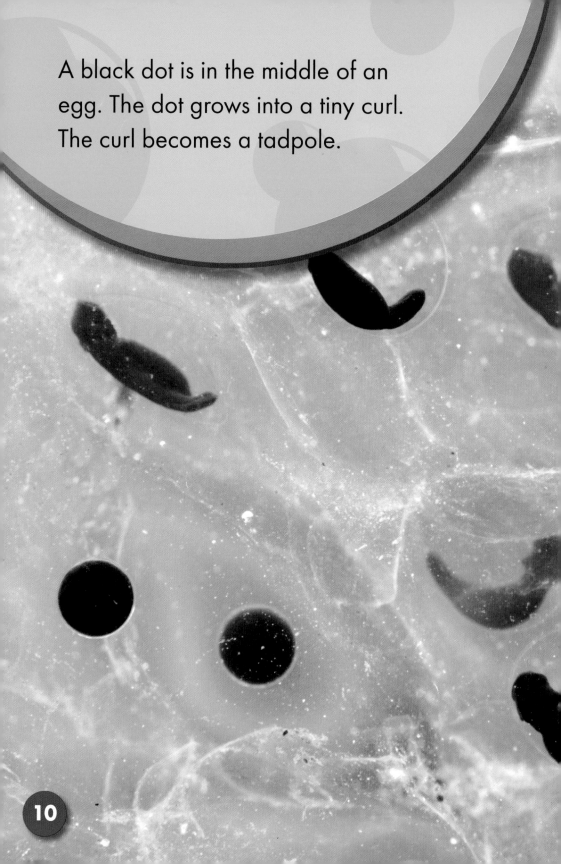

A black dot is in the middle of an egg. The dot grows into a tiny curl. The curl becomes a tadpole.

The tadpole is ready to hatch.
It breaks through the egg and
wiggles into the water.

The tadpole has a long tail for swimming.
It grows **gills** for breathing underwater.

The tadpole grows teeth. It uses the teeth to scrape **algae** off plants for food.

The tadpole grows bigger. It now has **lungs** instead of gills. It must swim to the surface to breathe air.

The tadpole grows two long back legs with **webbed feet**.

webbed feet

The shorter front legs grow inside the tadpole's body. The legs poke through the tadpole's skin when they are fully grown.

The tadpole climbs out of the water and hops onto shore. It is now a young frog.

The frog's tail gets shorter and shorter. One day it is gone. The tail has become part of the body.

The adult frog has big eyes and a wide
mouth. It snaps out its long tongue to
catch **insects** to eat.

The frog lives mostly on land now. Sometimes it dives into the water to cool off.

In a few years the frog finds a mate.
Each egg in their spawn is the start of
a new life cycle.

Glossary

algae—tiny living things without roots or stems that grow in water

amphibian—an animal with a backbone whose body temperature is the same as its surroundings; amphibians live in the water and on land.

croak—to make a low, rough sound; some frogs puff up their throats with air when they croak to make the sound louder.

fertilize—when an egg from a female joins with special cells called sperm from a male; a tadpole will grow only in an egg that has been fertilized.

gills—the organs on the sides of an animal that are used to breathe underwater

insect—a small animal with six legs and a body divided into three parts

life cycle—the stages of life of an animal; a life cycle includes being born, growing up, having young, and dying.

lungs—organs inside the body that animals use to breathe

mate—a male or female of a pair of animals

spawn—a large mass of eggs laid by amphibians; only a few of the thousands of eggs in a spawn will become adult frogs.

tadpole—a young frog that hatches from an egg and looks like a small fish; the tadpole stage is the second stage of a frog's life.

webbed feet—feet that have toes connected by thin, flat skin; webbed feet help frogs and tadpoles swim quickly in water.

To Learn More

AT THE LIBRARY

Huseby, Victoria. *Frog*. Mankato, Minn.: Black Rabbit Books, 2009.

Kalman, Bobbie. *The Life Cycle of a Frog*. New York, N.Y.: Crabtree Publishing, 2002.

Murray, Julie. *Frogs*. Edina, Minn.: ABDO Publishing, 2007.

ON THE WEB

Learning more about life cycles is as easy as 1, 2, 3.

1. Go to www.factsurfer.com.

2. Enter "life cycles" into the search box.

3. Click the "Surf" button and you will see a list of related Web sites.

With factsurfer.com, finding more information is just a click away.

Index